SOMEWHERE BETWEEN a ROCK and a HARD PLACE

SOMEWHERE BETWEEN a ROCK and a HARD PLACE

ROLAND DWAYNE GLOSSON

XULON PRESS

Xulon Press
2301 Lucien Way #415
Maitland, FL 32751
407.339.4217
www.xulonpress.com

© 2022 by Roland Dwayne Glosson

All rights reserved solely by the author. The author guarantees all contents are original and do not infringe upon the legal rights of any other person or work. No part of this book may be reproduced in any form without the permission of the author.

Due to the changing nature of the Internet, if there are any web addresses, links, or URLs included in this manuscript, these may have been altered and may no longer be accessible. The views and opinions shared in this book belong solely to the author and do not necessarily reflect those of the publisher. The publisher therefore disclaims responsibility for the views or opinions expressed within the work.

Unless otherwise indicated, Scripture quotations taken from the King James Version (KJV) – *public domain*.

Paperback ISBN-13: 978-1-66284-526-0
Ebook ISBN-13: 978-1-66284-534-5

TABLE OF CONTENTS

Purpose 1
Keep Striving Forward 9
No Reason to quit 17
Do not give up on Life's Problems 25
No Exceptions for Nice People 37
Ministering to the Needy 49
Solving Spiritual Battles Daily 55
Press on to Victory 67

Have you ever walked through a heavy fog and wondered what is in front of you? Have you ever seen yourself above ground but thought you were drowning? Have you ever felt that the deck was stacked against you? That is exactly how I felt going through life. The struggles had me ready to give up and just say this is not for me. I would constantly question the motives of God. The reasons why I had to go through this. Woah is me and this is so unfair. I had to really reevaluate my life and realize that I could no longer question what it is that God was doing; rather, why was he doing it? The Lord says that he does not put more on us than we can bear. During my life, I have encountered many different things that many would throw their hands up. Life begins as a mustard seed that must be watered. This book entails my struggles through portions of my life that God and only God has brought me through. Through this reading you will find strength in knowing that you are not alone. God sends an army and shields through the toughest obstacles. Reading through each chapter will challenge you to find inner strength and will to pray no matter what. Finding hope may be difficult and at times a struggle to even think of hope during the dark times; however, there is Power in his name. While you read this I will be praying that whatever storm you are facing that you will just drop to your knees and stop wondering why it is you and rather how you can be moved by the Lord.

Chapter One
PURPOSE

I WAS ON my knees during my Bible reading and praying, spending time with my Lord as I usually do, when I heard, "It's time you wrote a book." I asked God, "What should I write about?" and He said, "The struggles that I brought you through for many years." So, I got a spiral notebook, began to think back, and started writing what came to me

I prayed and the words started coming. Before I knew it, my fingers were so tired from writing, I had fallen asleep. So every day, I would pray and start writing all over again. It took many years to complete what I wanted in this book.

I was born in Southern Mississippi in a predominately Black state, but that didn't bother me at all. I went to school at Como Elementary during my first years until it was time to go to Greenhill Middle School where I was to complete the fifth through the eighth grade. I lived in a concrete house with my grandmother and her family members. As I matured, I ended up going back home with my mom, stepfather, and siblings where we lived in Sardis, Mississippi.

When I was first born, my stepdad convinced my mom to sell me to a couple in Ponotoc, Mississippi for one hundred dollars, two cases of beer, two rolls of barbed wire, and a 1955 Buick. But my grandmother came and got me with the police, and took me home where I lived until I became a teenager.

In the South, there was work and it was hard, but I managed because I had to in order to buy my school clothes and supplies. You see, my stepfather was angry because I was not his, and so he labled me the black sheep of the family. During the summer when I was out of school, I would work picking and chopping cotton for five dollars a day because he wouldn't buy anything for me. To put it blank, he hated me.

I had two brothers and two sisters named Jerry, Richard, Vilicia, and Carlene who I loved very much and a stepfather Jerry who was an alcoholic. He took everything that my mother worked for all week and would go out with his buddies and drink it all up. Then when he came back home, he would come in, kick her down to the floor, and start hitting her in the face. Blood would start running all over, even onto the floor. I saw him drag her by her hair down the hallway to the bedroom, and he would shut the door and begin to throw her everywhere. He would let us go to church where he would have the opportunity to beat upon my mom again, but when we returned home, he would whip me because he hated me. As time went by, I soon graduated middle school and then went to North Panola High where I attended for four years before graduating and receiving a diploma. I ended up enlisting in the United States Army where I went to Fort Dix, New Jersey for basic training and then on to Fort Knox, Kentucky for my accession training, or A School. My MOS, or job description, was a 63 November where I was a jeep driver and mechanic, and a 63 Foxtrot where I was a heavy equipment operator and a recovery man.

After my hitch was up, a friend asked me to go into the Navy with him, so we went to take the ASVAB Test to see what our job descriptions would be. I qualified as an airplane mechanic. A week later, the recruiter picked us up and drove us to Memphis, Tennessee to the hotel where we spent the night. We went to the station the next day, took a physical, and were sworn in.

They loaded everyone onto a bus after we were sworn in and were taken to the airport. We boarded a Delta jet for Orlando, Florida. It took a couple of hours before we landed and then we got onto another bus that took us to the base. We were taken to the processing station after we arrived and were issued our clothes, boots, and everything we needed for bootcamp. We were then carried to the dorm where we stayed for ten weeks before graduating and moving onto A School for our job training.

When we completed A School, we were handed our orders to where we would be stationed. Mine said that I would be going to the USS Saratoga where I would work as an aviation ordanceman. We were given a few days to go home and spend time with our families before going on to Norfolk, Virginia for shipboard fire fighting and training.

After we completed our training, we got into a friend's vehicle and drove to the Philadelphia Naval Shipyard where we would board the ship, which was in drydock going through a complete overhaul which would take approximately two years to finish. I can remember getting out of my friend's vehicle and looking up at this huge ship and thought to myself, How can this even float?

The ship had to be taken out for trials and tests once it was completed in order to be ready for war, in case it happened. After passing all tests, we loaded all vehicles, animals, furniture, and people, and headed for our homeport in Mayport, Florida where we spent the rest of our time and it took around 3 to 5 days to get there.

We ended up going on a cruise that would take six to nine months to complete in the Mediterranean Sea. We were guarding the United States against any other country that would harm us in any way. We had every type of weapon we needed to defend and airplanes of all types to carry them.

We would stay out for seven days at a time before pulling into a port for some well deserved "R and R." We pulled into Naples, Italy several times, and ports in Spain, France, Egypt, and Tunisa. The ship had five thousand men, two thousand pounds of groceries, and all types of weapons. You could say the ship was a floating city because it had stores to buy anything, a post office, a bank, a galley for eating, and berthing for sleeping.

My job had been as an aviation ordanceman, which meant I built bombs, missles, and mines which I would also quality inspect. I wanted to re-inlist for another six years, but something happened to keep me from it. I wrote to my senators and congressman when I returned home trying to get an answer, but never could.

CHAPTER TWO

KEEP STRIVING FORWARD

So I started looking for a job, with the Veterans Affairs' help, and ended up getting hired on at Cooper Tire in Tupelo, Mississippi.

My job was to make the product used to build tires, so I started out in the mixing section of the plant. I ended up working there for nine months before being hired by a pastor to remodel houses. I really enjoyed this type of work because my uncles and grandfather had taught me when I was young.

I ended up getting married to a country girl named Cathy, but it didn't last long because I was still wild from the service. I wasn't ready to settle down, we got a divorce, and I moved back home until I could find a place to live.

I turned my life around when I was invited to Cedar Grove United Pentecost, the church where my boss William White attended. I started going regularly and that was where I met a young lady named Christy Putt and We started dating and ended up getting married. She ended up pregnant with twins, but she lost them in the bathroom while at the factory where she worked as a sewing machine operator. We tried again and were successful the next time, giving birth to a baby girl who we named Cheyenne, and then another baby girl named Lashonda.

We were married for ten years before divorcing because she was cheating on me with different men and got on drugs really bad. She was on cocaine, marijuana, and there was no telling what else, and it was taking the money for our bills to afford her habit.

I stayed single for seven years; no dating at all, just going to work and to church. I worked in apartments and hotel maintenance for a period of thirty-one years before retiring with my wife Vicky now. I met her at the apartments where I was working as the maintenance supervisor. We dated for a while before marrying and she had 4 children from previous marriages named Beth, Suzy, Gage, and Brandi.

We moved to Thomas Street where we bought a home for us and our four children, two from her previous marriage and two from mine. We lived there for a couple of years and attended Word of Life Non Denominational Church where Pastor Tommy Galloway preached.

We found out that one of our oldest daughters had gotten sick with cancer, so we decided to move to San Antonio, Texas. My wife left three months earlier than me because we had to sell the house and get everything in order in Mississippi before I could leave. After I found a buyer and closed on the house, we rented a large Penske truck and our family and friends started loading our belongings. After we finished, we said our goodbyes and headed out for Texas. I drove all day and, just as it was getting dark, we had to make a stop at Fort Sam to let off our foster daughter named Amber to her dad who was waiting. My other daughter and I continued on our journey to San Antonio where we would meet up with the rest of the family.

We pulled into San Antonio early the next morning and the family had breakfast ready and we ate and went to sleep until late morning. The next day, I went exploring around the apartments where we were living and decided to go to the office and apply for a job there. I ended up being hired as a make ready, which was a person who would get the apartments ready to rent. Later, we found a church to attend called Livingway Church and We went there for a couple of years under the covering of Steve and Becky Fender. The apartments where we lived for six years were called Sable Ridge before moving to Millers Ridge where we rented a house.

My wife and I applied for a foster parent license, got it, and were put in charge of sexually abused teenage girls. When the girls came to us, usually all they had were the clothes on their backs and maybe a sack in their hand. This was because when the Children's Protective Service went to pick them up and the police were called, that was all they had time to get before being transported to a shelter for the night or foster home. We took in Jocelyn, Sofi and her daughter Atacella, Sara, and brother James.

When we would sit down and read their profiles, it would make us just cry for them because of the trauma they had endured by family members and close friends. So many people who foster are doing it for the money, but it's not about money at all because these kids have been through so much trauma.

You see, God calls certain people for certain tasks in life and this is one of them. When the kids came to us, we gave them love and attention and they got to learn about the Lord. We were over the youth and every month on a Sunday we would let them run every part of the service. They really enjoyed it, and it gave us a chance to win them to the Lord. A lot of kids don't have an opportunity to do this because Satan has them doing his duties. Most of them have joined gangs selling drugs, robbing, stealing cars, and even killing to get in. They take beatings, have to perform something bad, or are gang raped by every man or boy in the gang.

After doing street ministry while going to Livingway Church for a couple of years and winning souls for Jesus, we were praying one night and the Lord told us to start a church. We obeyed and started the church out of our home with our family and four couples from Livingway. The first service we had was awesome and we had an evangelist visit.

After the service, we had a time of fellowship and the evangelist shared what the Lord had been talking to him about. He told me that he had been praying for two years that God would send him somebody that would take over his radio broadcast. He said when the door to our home opened, he saw a light go straight toward me and God said, "There's the man that you have been praying for. I have equipped him for such a time for this type of ministry."

So we started going on the radio worshiping and preaching for souls to be won. We were on there for over nine months, and the owner of the station said his ratings went up over halfway after the first broadcast. Even though we had to drive an hour one way, it was a joy to minister and win souls for the Lord.

We kept having services in our home until we outgrew it and knew it was time to look for a building. We went out looking and couldn't find anything until a guy came up to me at a restaurant and asked me if I had found a building. I told him not yet, and he said he knew a friend who had a building we could get to worship in for nothing. We called him that night after he got home from work and talked to him about the building. He said it was ours if we wanted it, and we said yes. The next day, we drove over to pick up the keys so we could see what we needed to do in order to start worshiping there.

We had to build walls, paint, build a stage, and install lighting. Ater that, we had to get inspections done before we could move in and start having services at "Tree Of Life Christian Fellowship" and We needed a van to pick up the adults and kids who had no way of getting to us, so we prayed and asked God for one as well as the money to buy it. It was probably a week or so that we had a Ford Explorer pickup truck in our driveway that was given to us. It was just getting dark when a truck pulled up and the driver asked me if the pickup was for sale, and I said yes. To make a long story short, they gave me $12,00 for it. It was a week before Christmas and we had enough to buy a van that a guy had, plus money for Christmas gifts.

We passed inspections on the building and were ready to have church for the first time. We had a large group, around twenty or thirty people, and we worshiped the Lord and the souls we won for Jesus. I guess we probably worshiped there for about two or three months, until we were praying one night before going to bed and the Lord spoke a word that a pastor from a church needed help.

Chapter Three
NO REASON TO QUIT

So after praying and hearing His word, we got into our vehicle and drove down the street for about two or three miles until we saw a church. We pulled into the parking lot and we heard God say, "Here." We took down the name of the church and my wife called the next day. She spoke to the secretary and said that we needed to speak to the pastor. She was invited to his office where Gerald and his wife were and she told them what God had told us. It was right on time because they had also been praying for God to send them someone to work with the youth in the church.

We became the youth pastors of the church for a period of five years. We started going to the streets on Saturdays talking to kids and inviting them to come. Our youth group grew constantly and it was a joy to see the kids of all ages worshiping Jesus. They really enjoyed it because it wasn't boring; we had upbeat music and they danced all the ways they knew how. They even incorporated the dances they had learned on the streets.

After we got a large group to the church, we would load them up in the vans and go witnessing and ministering in the streets downtown. We went to where the homeless were staying, even where the gangs were. It didn't matter to us where we traveled because we always touched the hearts of the people. We would fix tacos of all kinds and take water to give to them while they worshiped at the service. Every time we went down there, we won many souls. People were delivered from drugs, alcohol, cigarettes, and just about whatever was prayed for.

I can remember one Saturday when I preached a message at the back of Sams ministry building where food was given out to the needy. It was titled "Double Reflection Of A Teenager" and, believe me when I say, it reached out to there's no telling how many people. When I gave them the invitation, they rushed to the edge of the stage with tears running down their faces. Many were saved for the Lord that day and they were also given the opportunity to be baptized. I was mentored by a pastor named David Kirk for a couple of years before being called as an evangelist. We ministered downtown San Antonio at the Samms shelter, Salvation Army, and under bridges where the homeless were. We reached many people of different races and we also carried food and water every time we ministered.

We also started a food ministry at the church and people came of all races to the service which lasted about an hour. They had to be in the service in order to receive food and many were won to the Lord because of this. You know, God works in mysterious ways and can work through anybody or anything. He used prostitutes, men who couldn't speak well, also a donkey to talk to a man. Young people are hard to reach during this season because the Devil makes everything look so sweet, but they don't realize that in the end, it's death in hell's fire.

The Bible says the Devil comes to steal, kill, and destroy. I can remember helping this couple move into an apartment. After awhile, we decided to take a break and there were some gang members in a circle talking and the Lord told me to go into the circle and start calling His name. So I obeyed Him and went into the circle, walking around and saying His name. As I was circling around, I could hear the members saying "This man is a fool" or "He is of God."

I heard God say, "Start praising Me," and so I kept obeying. All of a sudden, all of them left but one: the leader. He jumped up, reached behind his back, and pulled out a gun. He put it to my head and told me he was going to kill me, but I wasn't afraid of him at all. He cursed and tried his best to pull the trigger, but the gun wouldn't fire. He got frustrated at me and kept trying to fire the weapon until the magazine fell to the ground and he fell to his knees, pulled his colors off, and surrenderd to the Lord right there. A few Sundays later, we baptized him in the sweet name of Jesus Christ and he danced in that tub praising the Lord for I don't know how long. I kept in touch with him only to find out he had been called to the ministry.

There was another time when I was working one day in an apartment in the bathroom just praising the Lord when a little girl walked in, sat down, and started listening. I stopped and started telling her Bible stories and her mom was listening to the radio and I could hear the volume going down as I was talking to her daughter. I knew she worked at the strip club behind the apartments to put food on the table and to pay the bills. When I finished telling her stories and was walking toward the door, the radio volume went back up.

Maybe a couple of weeks later, I was pulling up to the apartment close to hers. When I got out of my truck and went to close the door, I saw a shadow to the side of me: it was the mother of the little girl on her knees just crying out. I walked over to her and led her to Jesus. This happened all of the time because I was given favor to witness for Jesus every opportunity that I had.

There's no telling how many people I have won for the Lord during my ministry while working all the years in the apartment and hotel industry. I thank Him for giving me favor over the management while working in this industry. Every opportunity that I get to tell somebody about Jesus, I take it because the Bible says we are not promised tomorrow and I don't want to see anyone go to hell. So we moved from the city to the country where we bought a double wide and we had land also to be cleared before moving on it. We looked for a church to attend and found one about 1 mile from our house called South Side Baptist where pastors Albert and Judy Byrum were with a large congregation. We were there for over seven years where we plugged into every area we could serve.

I remember one day after work while driving home, I started having chest pains and my breathing was short. I pulled off of the road, turned my truck off, called my wife, and told her I was dying. After that, I dropped the phone and passed out. It took them forty-five minutes to find me.

When they got me to the hospital, they said I had had a minor heart attack and they kept me there for seven days. Unfortunately, that was the end of working for me, so the next day, my wife called everybody we owed and said to come pick up their stuff, even the automobiles.

Chapter Four

DO NOT GIVE UP ON LIFE'S PROBLEMS

ALL WE COULD do was trust God from that point on. I was told by the doctors that I wasn't to be out in the heat at all because they said it would hurt me, too. We had around two acres of land with the house. I couldn't even mow the grass anymore, so it grew so tall you couldn't see the road on which we lived. On one side of the house, the electric quit working. It was tough, but we managed. We didn't have beds to sleep on, but we had two recliners we slept in for over two years. Our outside and inside heating and air units burned up midsummer when it was over 100 degrees outside. But the church that we were attending brought us two window units that had both heat and air, which was a blessing.

The hospital where I had my appointments was over forty miles one way. It was a VA hospital called Audie L. Murphy, and I had gone there for many years. The nurses and doctors were very nice and helped me with any problem that I encountered. I ended up having seizures, sometimes up to eight a day, but they managed to get me stabilized with medicine.

The Bible tells us that we can do all things according to Phillipians 4:13 and it also says that He would not put on us more than we can bear. You see, I got bored just sitting in the house day after day watching television or reading my Bible. It got to the point that I knew I couldn't provide for my family anymore, and I said to myself that there was no point in living.

I had always been the breadwinner in the family for many years and I felt like a nobody not being able to work anymore. So, my pastor called me for an appointment to talk about what was going on with me. I went and told him what was bothering me and he showed me in the Bible what God said about it and also prayed for me that day. Albert and Judy Byrom were the senior pastor and first lady in the church we were attending at the time, and you couldn't have asked for a sweeter group of people to be around for anything to do with the church.

The name of the church was South Side Baptist and had a large congregation. The people were very sweet; it didn't matter at all what we needed, they would take care of it. You see, before I got hurt, I was driving the church van, teaching Sunday school, helping out with the youth, and preaching every other Wednesday night. I was also part of the deacon board where we made major decisions concerning the church.

So we decided to make a move and ended up going to some part of Arizona.

We really enjoyed the church for seven years before we up and moved to Phoenix, Arizona. We rented two large U-Haul trucks and bought a fourteen foot landscaping trailer to put our animals in. We had church friends that started loading trucks with our belongings and it took several hours before we were done. After we loaded the trailer with hay and buckets for food and water for the animals, we pulled out around ten o'clock at night. We didn't drive far before we pulled into a Loves truck stop to rest for the night and get a fresh start the next day. We found a place to eat breakfast the next morning before pulling out on the highway again on the journey to Phoenix. We drove until noon before pulling off to eat lunch and to take a break from driving. Afterwards, we hit the highway again, drove until dark, and found another Loves truck stop to rest for the night. All in all, it took us three days to make the trip to Arizona, and we pulled in around ten o'clock at night on November 7, 2014. We were very tired, so we stayed in a Holiday Inn for the night. The next day, we drove down the road to find a cheaper place to stay while we searched for a place to live. After we found a place, we rented a room and rested for a couple of hours.

We then called around to find a vehicle that we could buy for a reasonable price. We went and bought a Volkswagon

Jetta station wagon that we could all fit into comfortably. After doing this, we loaded up and started looking for a house to rent. Unfortunately, this became a problem because people they called "snowbirds" were renting everything in sight or the houses they had rented before the owners were saving them.

After driving around for three days looking, we decided to just rent a hotel room for the month. We ended up staying at the Extended Stay Inn off of Interstate 17. We had everything furnished except for our laundry and food to eat. We stayed there while my wife and daughter were looking for a house or apartment to live in. Two weeks later, they found an apartment with a nice neighborhood, a swimming pool, and lots of emenities. We moved in and stayed for six and half months. Unfortunately our tax check was late coming back and the apartments told us we had to move. So we stored our stuff in the garage and went looking for a place to stay till our taxes came back. We had no money except a little for gas and food. but me being a disabled veteran contacted Boots for Troops and they paid our hotel fee.

◇◈◇

Our oldest granddaughter got sick and had to be admitted to Phoenix Children's Hospital. Her and her mom stayed for six months up there and the doctors ran every test they could just to diagnose her with the same disease as the little girl from the movie Miracles from Heaven about Anna Beam from Texas. Anna had to be flown to Boston to the pediatrics to see Dr. Nurko. He ran many tests and discovered she had what was called dysmotility, which is an intestinal disease where the stomach swells up so tight that it looks like a beach ball. You can't keep food down, not even water, so you have to have a feeding tube put through your nose in order to eat. You also have a peripherally inserted central catheter, or a PICC line, to your heart to monitor everything that is happening.

There are only five places in the U.S. that have the capability that specialize in this disease: Boston, Ohio, California, Dallas, and Atlanta. The doctor at Phoenix Children's Hospital told our daughter that they could no longer treat our granddaughter. We were then living in a suburb outside of Phoenix where we rented a four bedroom, two bath in El Mirage where we lived for three years. We were attending South Peoria Baptist under the covering of Pastor James and Anna Hayes at the time. We plugged into whatever ministry they needed help with while serving there until we had to make a urgent decision on where to go to for our granddaughter.

We ended up buying an RV that had been sitting for over six years, but I managed to get it running, so the owner sold it to us for $2,000. We drove it home, and the next day, we rented a U-Haul truck to move our belongings into a storage building until we could find a place to live in Georgia. Our daughter, son-in-law, and grandkids left for Georgia before we did because we had to finalize everything in Arizona.

Two weeks later, we hit the road, but decided to take it slow because we were going to stop and visit our daughters in San Antonio and Pflugerville, Texas before continuing on to Georgia. We visited them and then pulled out onto Interstate 10. We had a 2014 Volkswagon being pulled behind our RV. When we pulled into Vinton, Louisana to a Loves truck stop for fuel and to take a break, we used the restroom and bought some things to eat and drink on the way. We paid for the fuel and when we got back outside, our car was gone.

So, we fueled up the RV and pulled over to the side to park and called the police to make a report. When the police arrived and were filling out the report, they got a text from the sheriff's department in Rose, Texas. They said our car had been totaled and couldn't be repaired. We had to contact our insurance carrier and tell them what had happened. When the police finished with the report, we were free to hit the road again.

We drove on well into Mississippi where we found a Pilot truck stop to sleep at for the night. The next morning, we ate breakfast, fueled up, and hit the road again. We only had six hours before making it to Tifton, Georgia, so we arrived around five or six o'clock that evening. We pulled into a KOA Campground to spend a couple of days in order to give us time to find a place to live, but we left there and our daughter found an apartment to live in. We stayed there for three months before looking for a house in Augusta, Georgia.

We called around Augusta looking for houses only to keep getting denied, but one day, my wife Vicki was looking on her phone and happened to notice an ad for a house that was available for rent. We called and talked to the owner and rented it without seeing it.

While living in Tifton before moving to Augusta, my wife somehow managed to get ammonia in her body only to give her symptoms of dementia. So, one night around midnight, she woke up asking me who I was and I said your husband. She didn't remember anything, not even the grandkids' names at all. I took her to the hospital and she stayed one week before being discharged.

After she was released, we rented a small U-Haul and headed out toward Augusta. As we drove the RV, I noticed a funny smell like burning wires. I pulled off to the side of the highway to check it out and when I raised the hood, the RV caught on fire. We lost everything that day. Our daughter drove to the nearest town, rented a vehicle, and we headed out again.

We made it to Augusta around six o'clock that evening and moved into the house. In the Bible, God said He would supply all of our needs to His riches in glory, and He did so this time because the owner was a Christian realtor and we got the house for a great price. We got into our daughter's car one day and drove out to where the owner, named Jared Spivey, lived. He had a 2006 Mercedes Benz for sale and we asked him what he wanted for it. He said he had been trying to sell it for awhile, but it just wasn't the right time.

He told us he would take $5,000 for it and would let us pay $400 a month for twelve months. This is how God works because we didn't have the money at the time to pay straight out, and the house we got had four bedrooms, two baths, and a large inground swimming pool. The house was also only a mile or so from the Masters Golf Tournament, and we found a wonderful church to attend called Whole Life Ministries under the covering of Pastor Sandra Kennedy.

We went through the new members class for four weeks, then discipleship class for another four weeks before we could join the church and choose where we would like to serve. We were looking forward already to serve in the church wherever they needed us; we just wanted to serve the Lord, it didn't matter doing what. We had also been approached to be on Christian television with Dorthy Spaulding and her husband to tell our story of how the Lord had used us in ministry for the years we had.

Any time someone wants to do something for God, the enemy is going to try his best to stop them. We had been under heavy attack ever since we got the word about it, but we had a lot of people from churches everywhere covering us in prayer. Many of the friends and family members were also covering us. I hope in writing this book that it reaches just one person because then I know my job was completed.

Sure, it's been a long and rough journey, but without the Lord God's help, we would never have made it this far. He's taken us this far to not only leave us, but to carry us the rest of our journey, which I believe is just the beginning to what He has in store for us. We know we have to work while there's light because He's coming back soon to take us home; this is only our temporary home as we eagerly wait for His triumphant return.

Chapter Five
NO EXCEPTIONS FOR NICE PEOPLE

So many people are going about their everyday duties like nothing is going to happen. People are marrying and given in marriage, they're doing all kinds of immoral things, like they were doing in Sodom and Gomorrah. Things like homosexuality, pornography, idolatry, horemongers, fornication, and drunkerds. The people didn't believe that the flood was going to take place and kept making fun of Noah when God told him to build the ark. But when the rain started and Noah shut the door, they were screaming for Noah to open the door and he didn't, even while men, women, and children were drowning.

And that's the way it is, now, here on Earth because people who do not know Jesus don't think that there's a hell waiting for them, but it will be too late when He returns and says, "Depart from me, you worker of inigity, because I never knew you." And there, cast into the burning flames of hell, is where they will burn forever. The pain will be agonizing and unberable.

The saints of God, however, who are ready to meet Him will be caught up in the air with Him, and will later hear, "Well done, my good and faithful servant." Just think of those who are left behind during the tribulation period. It will be a time of pain because those who don't love God, their heads will be cut off like a martyr. The only way you will be able to buy and sell is if you take a mark of the beast on either your forehead or your right hand. This mark will read "666" so that you can be identified.

It says in the Bible that whoever taketh the mark when we come back with Jesus, they will become as a green boil or sore, and this is the way Jesus will know who took the mark. You will be living under a one-world government. You will also have to go into hiding in order to read the Bible and pray because you will be killed for even saying the name of Jesus. Your family will be tortured in so many ways that you can't even fathom.

So, please, get right with Jesus before it's too late. I'm pleading with you; don't wait, do it now so you don't have to be left behind. Tell your friends, neighbors, and anybody you come into contact with to turn around and repent. There are many signs now pointing to His return, like blood-red moons, and rivers and lakes turning to blood.

The Bible tells us in 2 Chronicles 7:14, that if we would seek God's face, turn from our wicked ways, and humble ourselves, than He would hear from heaven and heal our land. We need to seek God more than ever before because if we let the enemy come in and steal our joy and blessings, he will take over our lives.

We need to make a declaration to God every day that we are going to better ourselves because He says we can. We can do what He says we can do, we can have what He says we can have, and we can be what He says we can be. Prayer is the key to everything that we need, along with faith. The Bible tells us in the Book of Hebrews, that faith is the substance of things hoped for and the evidence of things not seen. In other words, if you believe, in your heart, that Jesus Christ died on the cross, and on the third day rose from the dead, this is as clear to the point as you probably could put it.

Praying constantly and effectual or fervently meaning intercession which, to me, means if there is a need with someone or something. If we come with an open heart and mind before the Lord and humble ourselves before His throne and be bold and no fear than we can expect the prayer to complete what it was called for in the first place. The Bible tells us in 1 Thessalonians 5: 16-18, to rejoice always, pray without ceasing, give thanks in all circumstances; for this is the will of God in Christ Jesus for you.

A lot of people pray, but never thank God for what He has done or for what He will do. Many times, we become discouraged because we don't know what else to say to the Lord. You see, when we stay in a place for a period of time in prayer, God is able to speak to us and clarify what He's teaching us. Romans 8:27 says, "And he who searches hearts knows what is the mind of the Spirit, because the Spirit intercedes for the saints according to the will of God."

So, what does it mean to pray without ceasing? It means to pray as often as we can, about everything we can. When was the last time you missed a meal because you prayed? When was the last time that you prayed late at night because you were burdened down about something? When was the last time you awoke early in the morning to seek the face of God?

You remember that Nehemiah prayed with a kind heart, desire, and persistence. And so, in turn, God answered his prayers in mighty ways. Colossians 4:2 states to continue steadfastly in prayer, being watchful in it with thanksgiving. Persisitence prayer takes faithfulness and patience. Also, if you're knocking on heaven's door now in anticipation of God answering a real life request in your life, you can rest assured that He hears you.

Remember in Luke 11: 5-10, Jesus offers a lesson in persistence through a parable. "He said which of you who has a friend will go to him at midnight and say to him, would you lend me three loaves for a friend has arrive on a journey; and I have nothing for him, and he will say don't bother me the door is shut, and my children are now in bed. And I can't get up and give you anything. Ask and it will be given; seek and you will find; knock and it will be opened." You see, Jesus is showing us that God disires to give good things to His children, unlike the man who wouldn't help his friend.

Persistence prayer means praying through doubt, fears, and always refusing never to give up; praying for certain things to happen even when He may have a better plan for you. Praying believers can change the destinies of men and women in other nations, even when we don't understand the purpose and the value of prayer when praying for such things as "God bless my family or my friends."

So pray in such a way that when God answers your prayer, you know without question what He said! Praying with boldness is not a "lay me down to sleep" prayer, it's not a "bless my food" prayer. It's a mighty prayer in the name of Jesus. You see, in my experience of prayer, God does business with those who mean business with Him. May we pray shamelessly and with passion. It costs blood, sweat, and tears to pray boldly, to bruise knuckles when asking, seeking, and knocking, but it's worth it because when we pray, God moves.

The Bible tells us in Hebrews 4:16 that we should come boldy before the throne of God and receive mercy and grace in times of need. In the Christian life, there is a balance between the Word of God and prayer. It's impossible to know what God wants us to do until we know what He first said in His Word. The will of God has been revealed in the Bible, and we must invest time for reading and meditating on the Word of God. In John 15:7, He tells us if we abide in Him, and His words abide in us, we will ask what we desire, and it will be done for us.

While it may not be feasible to study God's Word all day long, we can reflect on what we have read as we go on about our day. You know, God loves it when we call upon Him and when we use His Word. He has blessed His Word not only when it's preached and proclaimed, but also when it's prayed. The most effective prayer is the person whose filled with His Word.

Over the years, we have learned how to pray the Scriptures personally. For example, in Proverbs 3:5-6, "The passage about if we will trust the Lord with all thine heart and lean not to your own understanding, but in all your ways acknowledge Him and He shall direct your path." If you need God to come through in a powerful way to meet a need in your life, just pray Phillipians 4:19, "Lord I know that you are my God and you will supply all my needs to your riches in glory in Jesus Christ."

Perhaps one of the greatest ways to experience the power through prayer is intercession. You know that the enemy aims his big guns at the leaders, and many are hurt, discouraged, and even falling back to sin. So, we as God's people need to pray for pastors, Christian leaders, and the missionaries in America and around the world.

My wife and I know what it's like to be under attack because both of us are ministers of the Lord. We have been persecuted, cursed out, and even spit upon. We know what it's like to be in leadership because we've pastored and evangelized in just about every church we have represented throughout our many years of ministry.

We need to cry out to God for America, and if you love this country, pray for God to revive the church. Pray God will renew the families and also our communities in which we live. We need to pray for our neighbors and also our officials in offices. You see, prayer is not getting our will done in heaven, and it's not getting God's will here on Earth. He will give us what we need in His own way and in His own time. Nothing is out of reach of prayer except that is out of the will of God. Prayer is not changing His mind, but finding His mind. The way to learn what God wants in our lives is to pray.

In John 5:14-15, "This is the confidence we have in Him, that if we ask anything according to His will, He will hear us. But if we know that He hears us , whatever we ask of Him we know that we have petitions with Him." Day by day, we see that God reveals His will, and shows the way to the ones who truly seek Him and ask Him. I've come into contact with many people who seek the will of God and they want what they want, but what God wants for us may be a different path or plan.

In Psalms 143:10, it says "Teach me to do your will, for you are my God! Let your Spirit lead me on to level ground." Seeking the will of God is asking that we conform to the will of God. And yes, God still moves today in powerful and incredible ways. When we are faithful in our prayers, we will begin to notice changes in our lives. Prayer empowers us to be better friends, better spouses, better parents, better business parteners, and better people overall. The more time that we spend on our knees in the presence of God, the more we will experience peace, hope, and joy filling out our days on Earth.

If we were to ask what most people want in prayers, I would be willing to bet you it would be answers. You will see that, sometimes, God's answer will be quick, while other times it may be delayed. You will see that if you have a pressing need today, know He isn't holding out on you; just pray and wait on the answer. When we are faithful to observe God's instructions for our lives, then He is faithful to bless us as only He can. Note that prayer is not a substitute for obedience, nor is it an excuse for being lazy. Prayer makes us part of the answer.

Psalms 40:8 says, "I desire to do your will, O my God; your law is within my heart." We need to rise up from the place of prayer and to move forward in the spiritual service in obedience of God. You know that our goal must not be to discover His will, but to do His will. When we get on our kness regularly and consistently to read His Word and talk to Him and also listen to Him, He brings things to mind and we can bring glory to Him to support the work of Jesus Christ.

Some just say that I'm waiting on the Lord to show me what I'm supposed to do. Others say when He shows me, then I will do it. You know, I've found in my own life that God is actually waiting on me most of the time. A lot of times, He's usually waiting on me to pray, to get up from that place of prayer, and to act in the power of the Holy Spirit.

Are you praying dilengently? Are you then doing what He's calling you to do? Do you know that behind the scenes, there is a battle being fought for the very hearts and lives of women, men, and children across the world? There is an invisible war that is being waged between good and evil; between God and a created being known as Satan. We as believers are also already in a battle, and we're in it until the very end.

In Matthew 6:13, "And lead us not into temptation, but deliver us from evil." We are solidiers on a mission and the only way to win this war is to prepare and to pray. When we pray, we are protecting our faith, our future, and our families. When we're faced with temptation, our natural reaction is often to run to the world for solutions or we fight the best we can with our own flesh. We do everything except pray and ask God to deliver us!

In this season, we must remember that we are fighting a spiritual battle which can only be won with spiritual weapons that God has already provided. We must turn to God for strength in times of temptation, and He realizes the pressure we're experiencing in this season more than ever. You see, in a world filled with temptation, we have a stronghold against the enemy because God is our deliverer.

In closing, always remember to pray daily for the power of Jesus Christ in your daily life to deliver you. This will prevent the many struggles in all of our lives and the problems we face in this season!

Chapter six

MINISTERING TO THE NEEDY

We also went and ministered to the kids who were in gangs in every part of the city where they hung out. A lot of people told us that we were crazy for going to where they were, but everybody has a soul. There were kids of every age in these gangs. It was all they knew and they considered each other their family. Because most of them didn't have a parental figure in their lives at the time they joined the gangs. Most of their fathers or mothers were in jail or prison serving time for crimes that they had committed. Some were even strung out on drugs of every kind or working late jobs to make ends meet in order to put clothes on their backs and food on the table.

Most of the young girls were being used to make money for a lady or a man who was called their pimp. It was a shame to see them on the streets doing this because most of the kids were runaways from different places. And the reason they were doing this was because they couldn't get the attention or love from their fathers. So these pimps would buy them beautiful clothes to wear, and makeup and jewelry to make them look good so that men would pick them up and have their way with them.

But it wasn't just young girls; it was young boys, as well. These people would host parties and they would invite very important men and women from everywhere to pay money to have a good time with these girls and boys. These groups would go to different countries and pose as photographers looking for models. The young girls and boys would come to sign up and then be carried away to rooms thinking they were coming to the United States to become models for magazines. They would given their airplane tickets where they would be flown to a city, hoping to better their families, but would end up being sent to brothels or sweat shops to be used for sex.

This ended up being called human trafficking, where the youth were sold on the internet like slaves to the highest bidder. They were beaten many times for not wanting to participate for what they were asked to do. When they weren't working, they were locked in a room where they were sleeping on worn-out mattresses. A lot of times, they were given drugs and alcohol before taken to motels, casinos, and other places where they were paid to perform different sexual acts. Sometimes, we would reach one or two for the Lord and get them off of the streets and back to their families, but that was very rare.

It broke my heart to see them out there because it made me think about the young girls we were fostering and also my own daughters. We had an opportunity to raise some kids off of the streets and gave them a chance in life. If we hadn't, they could have ended up like those already spoken about.

A lot of times, we would see young kids as young as eight years old selling drugs on the street to provide for their families. There were many kids on drugs who were addicted who God delivered them away from. While ministering in the streets, it was common to see people shaking because they needed a fix. They would sell everything that was worth something in order to buy crack, cocaine, heroine, marijuana, or whatever pill that would make them high. Their bodies were like skeletons because of using drugs for so long and they looked like walking death.

Chapter 7
SOLVING SPIRITUAL BATTLES DAILY

While there, we looked for a house to live in somewhere out of the city area. We were praying and asking God to lead us to the right one that He wanted us to live in. We were contacted by a realtor to come look at one in the suburb of El Mirage, about thirty minutes outside of Phoenix. When our money finally came in, we moved and it was exactly what we had prayed for and more'

In the Bible, the Lord said that He would never leave us or forsake us in any manner, and that's the gospel truth. In His Word, He said He would supply all of our needs to His riches in glory, and many times, that's just what He did. He's called our Jehova-jireh, which means our provider. A lot of times, we ran out of food and didn't have money to pay our bills. We would reach out to resources within the area and pray and the Lord would make a way when there seemed to not be one.

You see, we have to find a place every day and take out time to pray and read His Word. Because if we don't, then we won't have the means needed to stand against whatever the enemy would come with. The Bible also tells us we must die to this flesh daily and take up our cross and follow Him. It tells us in Romans 3:9, "For we have all sinned and come short of the glory of God." Meaning unless we're born again and know Jesus, then we are no better than they are.

Proverbs 3:3-6 states that we should, "Trust in the Lord and lean not to our own understanding and acknowledge his ways and shall direct our steps." Romans 12:1-2 says, "We must be Living Sacrifices to God, I beseech ye therefore brethren by the mercies of God, that you present your bodies a living sacrifice, holy, acceptable to God, which is your reasonable service. And do not be conformed to this world but be ye transformed by the renewing of your mind, that you may prove what is that good and acceptable will of God."

Galatians 5:16-18 tells us, "I say then Walk in the Spirit and you shall not fulfill the lust of the flesh. For the flesh lust against the Spirit, and the Spirit against the flesh: and these are contrary to one another, so that you do not do the things you wish. But the fruit of the Spirit is love, joy, peace, longsuffering, kindness, goodness, faithfulness, gentleness, self-control, such there is no law."

In this season, there are so many people falling from God who have been in the ministry for many years. They are giving up on God and running back to their old lives because they say it's hard to reach people anymore. Everybody just wants to come to church just to be seen and say, "I came," but that doesn't work. The Lord says in His Word that if you're lukewarm, He will spew you out of His mouth. You need to be cold or hot. You can be a man or woman of God, but good works won't get you into heaven.

A lot of times, I think back to the little old white-haired ladies and men in church. The prayer meetings that would last all night or way into the morning or the revivals that would go for months. When you delight yourself in the Lord, when you listen to Him, when you look to Him, and linger in His presence, then God begins to implant His desires on your heart. He begins to change your desires to match His.

Prayer not only changes things, it changes us. It changes our attitude and our priorities. It is encouraging to know that we are not heard because of the language of our prayers, the length of our prayers, or the logic of our prayers, but because of the life that prays before God. It's not your words that matter, it's the genuineness of your heart. God is listening for people whose lives are transparent before Him, who are laid out before Him. God is looking for honest, genuine prayer warriors. But most of all, He wants you.

We can't expect God to bless our lives and those who we are praying for if we have hatred and malice. Sin is serious business to God and, therefore, should be serious to us. You see, if there's anything in our lives clogging God's channel of prayer in our lives, then we need to go before God, confess our sins, and ask for forgiveness.

Maybe some of you out there are thinking that I would be an absolute hypocrite to pray and that I have gone too far down to receive forgiveness, but let me remind you that the angels in heaven rejoice over one sinner who repents. It's time to quit beating yourself down, to get away from the guilt that you keep inside, and give it to the Lord and never pick it back up.

Have you ever been to a football game and played and you know that when you're down on the field, you can't see the plays developing? In the same way, sometimes we're too close to our own problems: we're right in the middle, and we can't see what is even happening. We need a clearer vision, a new perspective, so we need to get up higher! We need to get lifted up in the presence of God and gain a new perspective for His will and wisdom for our lives. We need to submit ourselves in prayer and get more hungry for the Lord.

His wisdom to us in James 1:5. It says, "If any of you lacks wisdom, let him ask God, who gives generously to all with reproach, and it will be given him." He's not only interested in our spiritual lives, but our physical and material lives, as well.

You see, the main concern of the Devil is to keep us from praying because he fears nothing from prayerless studies, prayerless word, or prayerless religion. It's like being in a wrestling match with him; he doesn't like to lose at all. God not only gave us prayer for worship and work, prayer is warfare! That's why God gave us a powerful weapon in prayer to be used as a covering, a source of strength, and a means to stand firm in the fiercest of battles.

1 Corinthians 10:12 tells us, "Let anyone who thinks that he stands take heed lest he fall." In other words, we need His strength and protection every day to combat the Devil's schemes. Through prayer, we have the invisible energy and the invisible force which is the key to our victory. It tells us in 2 Chronicles 7:14, "If my people who are called by my name, will humble themselves and pray, and seek my face and turn from their wicked ways, then will I hear from heaven and heal their land."

Prayer is hard work, and it is mental and spiritual discipline to our body and mind when we need it. He serves as our shield, our fortress, our strength, our deliverer, our strong tower, and a very present help in times of need. As God's children, we must constantly monitor our heart's posture to be sure our motivation for entering His presence is pure.

Having a sincere heart before God means refraining from running into His presence with each day's shopping list. Instead, be slow and quiet and express how humble God is. Sincere prayer is not about the physical position in which you would pray, but about the spiritual attitude toward your heart. God said when you go to pray, go to your room, shut the door, and pray to Him in secret and He will reward you for it. We need to draw close to Him every chance we have because someday soon, we may not be able to.

The Bible tells us that we are not promised tomorrow, another day, hour, or second, but says there's going to be a trumpet sound so loud it will wake the dead and He will split the eastern sky and we will be caught up with Him.

In this season, we're too busy running and not taking time to see what's happening around us. We should be called "microwave Christians." We're like fast food restaurants where we go to church, see what the menu has for the day, and then sit down and eat what's prepared for that service. People just don't have time for God anymore. They get what's served, then get into there vehicles and go down the road to see what's served somewhere else. They don't want the real truth anymore; all they care about is a sermon to make them feel good.

Churches don't preach about hell anymore. That's the reason their packing the people in and filling their pockets with money. They're building these mega buildings and telling people that all they have to do to be healed is send in some money and the church will them send some water. Or if people will continue to send money, the church will mail them a piece of cloth.

If you want to see people set free from the bondage and chains that have them bound, there needs to be one of those old-fashioned tent revivals that last for months. The Devil can't stand it because he knows a lot of folks are going to be made whole from the sin they're hiding and don't want anybody to know about. But you can't hide anything from God because He is all-seeing and all-knowing. Just like when we're at our computer working and a pop-up keeps coming on time after time, asking you to just click on it. You know that the enemy will make something look so good just to make you want to click that button.

You know that pornography is one of the main ways to break a relationship or a wonderful marriage apart. The Bible says that the enemy comes to steal, kill, and destroy anything he can use against us. There are so many men hooked on pornography because they have subscriptions to magazines that come in the mail every month. There are also youth pastors who have these magazines hidden in their office in the bookshelf with other magazines.

The reason that I can say this is because when I was a young boy, that's where I found out about it. Men hide them under the seats of the vehicle in which they drive every day, hoping no one will find them. They also hide them under the mattress, the bathroom sink, behind the toilet, in the work place, under the desk, hunting blinds, and anywhere else they could think of. The reason I know is because I was hooked on pornography for a period of five years before I was set free from it. But I can testify today that I do my best to help people with this problem get free from it because it's like a cancer that eats you inside and out.

But there's a God out there when things like this happen. It breaks His heart in two and sets at the right hand of the Father shedding many tears. Another is living the life as a battered wife or girlfriend hiding behind their makeup so no one can see the bruises, or wearing dark sunglasses to cover black eyes. Men want women to submit like a slave this day and time, not letting them go anywhere by themselves, or not letting them call or go see their families.

If walls could talk, what would they tell us? Maybe pictures moved around to cover the holes where a head went through, or furniture moved to cover up the blood that was spilled and dried everywhere, or curtains pulled to hide the broken window panes. What about all of the language coming from the mouth of adults that children shouldn't here? But these women are supposed to be treated like the brides of the church. And when you're at the altar saying those vows to the one beside you, "for better or for worse till death due you part," that's just what it means.

I am saying this because your mate could be in an automobile crash tomorrow, be bedridden, and may not look like they did before the crash. Or you may have to wait on them hand and foot, or maybe have to learn to braid their hair, bathe them, and feed them. How many would take the vows serious these days? I tell you, not many.

Many of us today are living in a world filled with spiritual darkness. People are all about grasping for something to bring light into their darkened lives. We are not in the same places. Some of us are in far away places, others in their families, neighborhoods, and places of business. Sometimes, we are in such a dark place, we think that our small light cannot be seen. Isaiah 49:5-6 and 2 Corinthians 4:4-6 remind us of this often in our lives.

What would you do today if your best friend told you that you needed to endure a long, intense, and different trial so that God could prime away some of the sin in your life? You would probably think they were crazy. But they insisted and said you would perform your job as a mother, wife, husband, or a friend better after the trial was over. Which of us would willingly submit to the pruning shears and which of us would turn, run, and hide? When was the last time you felt "pressed"?

Perhaps it was when your mother suddenly came to live with you and your responsibilities and work load at home increased dramatically. Or maybe when your boss passed you over for a promotion because he didn't think you were working hard enough. Pressing can be painful and also profitable.

CHAPTER 8
PRESS ON TO VICTORY

I THINK BACK to one time following days of drenching rain, killer floods, and general chaos, there came a freak downpour. Without warning, a black curtain of rain simply swallowed our city up. I waded through a lake that came to the hem of my pants while trying to find my car in the parking lot. I then drifted to the front door of my house and heard children screaming like banshees, a dog demanding to be fed, a wife cheerfully announcing that the roof was leaking in five places, and the septic tank was overflowing. I had said, "Just let me in the door, please." So, we began the evening and hopped into the bed around midnight, the kids giggling, the roof still leaking into pans and buckets. I said the septic tank will just have to wait until tomorrow.

I woke up and realized the power was off. I looked out the window and realized that we had slept all night and into the next because the clock was off. We didn't have a way to tell what time it was. My boss was mad at me, but there was nothing I could do. All I could do was explain what had happened and the reason I couldn't make it to work.

There were times in my life that I can remember, but nothing compared to what Jesus Christ went through for us. I recall in Romans 5:3-4 that suffering produces perseverance, character, and hope. For me, suffering produced times of physical and emotional weakness after losing our twins from my first marriage as I lay near death myself. I tried to pray, but I was in shock and heavily medicated and no words would come into my mind. Later, I asked God why He took our children from us, but never received one answer.

You see, a major part of a Christian's journey is learning how to handle those times. When the heavens were locked, when our lives were weighed down with despair, pain, worry, and loss, we tried desperately to convince ourselves that we don't serve a God who has aborted Himself the listening post. Who has put up a closed shop sign and taken off for vacation somewhere. But the Lord proved to me over and over that His favor and grace are plentiful. He gave me wisdom and love as I sought to help young people handle their problems of daily living in the midst of poverty.

Christianity isn't a narcistic that dwells you into obedience it involves battle-tis excruciating to give up control. But that is why we must not feel despair if we are struggling. To struggle does not mean we are incorrigible; it means we are alive. Heaven will not be filled with its innocent people running around asking, "Oh, was there another way?" I guess we have noticed as we group in darkness, what do we want most? Light and direction. Darkness reminds us of our oppressive and burdensome need and it feels heavy even though it's intangible. Only light, which is also intangible, pushes that feeling away, It provides relief and lets us pursue that which is good, right, and truthful by shining through our darkened circumstances.

Don't keep the switch off or hold back as though our batteries have run down because our source is glorious light that pleases the Lord. The marriage and divorce rates have skyrocketed even when family life is rapidly deteriorating. Families need to be strong this day and time. My wife and I have been teaching family life seminars for many years, but most of the books that we have taught from have some form of family life. We have come across almost every problem possible in marriage and family relationships, and we still believe it is possible to have a strong family life and marriage relationship. The Word of God is used as the armor in order to withstand every trial that comes about in our lives. We must use the Word of God as our basis for sorting out right from wrong for making decisions and resolving conflicts.

It feels like the people in the world today are trying every avenue to take God out of everything. They have even changed the institution of marriage from the constitution saying women can marry women and men can marry men.

There are also girls born as females wanting to change themselves to males, and males wanting to become females. It's a shame how our society has turned out in this century and we have a president who stands for what's right, but is having a battle with Democrats and the news media.

He's done so much good for our country already, bringing unemployment to the lowest it's ever been, bringing businesses back to our country from overseas, making sure that veterans are to be first, and health insurance where everyone can afford it. The Democrats are doing everything possible to impeach this man from office, but God put him there with help of all evangelicals and no man will remove him until God is ready. You just keep trying and you will have a battle on your hands unlike anything you have ever seen in any war so far. He's making peace with other countries and that's a good purpose in this time, because God is working through him in bringing the darkness to light and exposing what is evil.

The reason our government has gotten away with it for so many years is because our crooked judicial system have turned their backs to people getting paid underhanded, immoral acts that have taken place in the White House, the Capitol building, and where else they could hide it. People in high offices taking vacations and using the money to pay for them when they make thousands of dollars. People in the government, like Hillary Clinton, getting by with murder and no telling what else. Nancy Pelosi and Chuck Shumer and all the things that they are getting away with today. All of these people who I have already mentioned who are corrupt and getting by need to be tried and convicted.

On November 5, 2017 during church services, a gunman from New Braunfels, Texas got into his vehicle with clips of ammo, a 9mm, and a rifle on a mission to kill his mother-in-law, but she wasn't there that day. He parked down the street at the BP gas station and got out with weapons fully loaded and proceeded toward the church. Now this was a small town in Sutherland Springs, Texas, and as he walked, he shot down the church security first, and then continued toward the doors of the church. He then opened the doors and started firing into the congregation, shooting anyone he could see.

After it was over, he had killed twenty-six, including the pastor's daughter. He made it back to his vehicle and proceeded to drive away, but neighbors jumped in a truck with guns and proceeded to chase him before firing at him and killing him. He was an Air Force veteran and they had let him slip through the cracks because he had been in trouble for domestic violence on his wife. All of this could have been prevented if they had reprimanded him on this matter while in service. He wouldn't have been able to purchase weapons or ammo that he used to carry out this heinous act on these people.

That's why the Veterans Affairs, or VA, is pushing stricter background checks now and banning fully automatic weapons, and magazines used for them. The VA has fired so many doctors because of veterans not getting the right care needed to get a handle on this matter. Many veterans have also died while waiting on medical lists, waiting to get the healthcare needed to survive. They have changed up and instituted a program called First Choice where a veteran can go and get outside care instead of the VA. There are between ten to twenty-five committing suicide daily because they can't handle transitioning back from combat to civilian life. There are so many diagnosed with PTSD, anxiety, and depression who have had a hard time dealing with the problems from the war with flashbacks and nightmares.

I had to take medicine to cope with everyday life just as other veterans who came back from the war. I think back to the day when a gunman walked into Sandy Hooks Elementary killing kids and teachers inside the hallway and then in the classrooms and back outside. Also, the Columbine school massacre and the guy who walked into a Florida high school when the doors were not locked, opening fire on the students and faculty. His parents were dead and he was living with foster parents where he found a gun to do what he had done because he had problems that no one knew about. He was shot and taken by ambulance to the nearest hospital where he was placed under guard.

Also, remember back to the young man who burst into a church when they were in Bible study and started shooting people before some of the men there took him down and held him until police could arrive. Or when the shooting took place at a movie theater in Oklahoma or the shooting at a nightclub in Florida killing many inside and outside. Or on a Sunday afternoon in San Antonio at the mall, where a gunman opened fire on innocent people and many were killed in cold blood, but a civilian with a concealed weapon took a shot at the gunman before he got away.

Recently, my life has been filled with changes. When you're getting old, you just can't do the things you used to do as well as you did. Your eating habits change and your social habits also change; you don't want to go and do things with people like you did. You just don't want to deal with the public anymore. A lot of people just want to shut themselves in, and just give up and die, but we need to encourage people to continue to get up and go out be around people.

I hope this book will reach out to someone to give them the ability to not give up, but to light a fire under them and burn forever. This book will help you to overcome the struggles in your life if you will let it. Everything that I have written, I know someone has had a challenge one time or another like them. The fact is the struggles that I talk about somebody has gone through. Many of you face them daily in life.

We need to press on toward the finish line, but in a race, only one will cross it and receive a reward or prize. When we have run the race with faith, and God says, "Well done, my good and faithful servant," that's what I'm waiting to hear. I can't wait to walk through those pearly gates and walk on those streets of gold. It's going to be a celebration we will never forget.

In closing, I thank God for giving me the opportunity to write the book. And may it bless all who read it and receive inspiration from it. And may God get the praise and glory which He deserves.